Sugarpaste / Rolled Fond[ant]

For ease of handling and consistency of product it is generally accepted that most businesses will use a commercially manufactured ready to use sugarpaste. These products all vary in consistency, taste, handling abilities and colours and therefore it is essential to understand your chosen paste.

Basic Tips

When covering a cake with sugarpaste use either icing sugar (powdered sugar) for dusting or roll the paste onto a surface covered with a very thin layer of white margarine (shortening)

Other mediums or dusting powders e.g. cornflour (cornstarch), may encourage fermentation and create problems at a later time.

To achieve the best finish when coating a cake it is normally an advantage to use fresh sugarpaste.

Colouring sugarpaste - ideally prepare this in advance. This will not only allow the paste to rest prior to use but also give the opportunity to check for unmixed spots of colour that may become visible after a period of time. Using dried or crusted food colour can often be a false economy as this may result in colour spots.

Ensure that all food colours conform to the required food standards. Remember that a small quantity of coloured sugarpaste can also be added to white sugarpaste to create a paler tint, or that different colours of sugarpaste can be blended together to create a new colour e.g. blue and yellow will create green. Use the colour wheel as a guide.

Ensure that all sugarpaste is kept well wrapped and stored ideally in a cool dry atmosphere.

In cold weather or if the storage temperature is cold, the sugarpaste may become difficult to handle, so place at room temperature prior to use.

Check the best before dates - Although purchasing in large quantities may offer an initial lower cost price, that advantage will be lost if the product exceeds its recommended use by date. Purchasing a little an often may be more cost effective in the long term

Adding Gums & Blending with Flowerpaste / Gum Paste

The formulation of manufactured sugarpastes vary considerably and therefore although there are basic guidelines regarding these additions and blends, adjust and adapt the paste according to your requirements. Have the confidence to work with pastes that are right for you and achieve the creative finish that you have designed.

Remember that sugarpaste can be flavoured if required, although this will also require balancing and co-ordinating with the cake flavours.

Simple Sugarpaste

icing sugar - sifted 500g (1lb)
liquid glucose 30ml (2 tablespoons)
white vegetable fat 25g (1oz)
egg white 25 - 50g (1 - 2oz)

Place the icing sugar, glucose and white fat into a bowl and begin mixing together.
Add the egg white a little at a time, enough to bind the ingredients.
Turn the paste out onto a work surface and gently knead until smooth and silky. Use icing sugar for dusting if necessary.
Store in an air tight plastic bag.

Coloured Sugarpaste

The versatility of sugarpaste, naturally encourages the use of colour. Food colourings are available in various forms e.g. liquid, paste, jel and powder. To add colour to sugarpaste aim to choose a concentrated paste or jel colour, this reduces the quantity of colour required and allows the

icing to be coloured without bec[oming...]
these colours is with a cocktail st[ick...]
To colour large quantities of suga[r...]
first in a deeper shade than requ[ired...]
the paste.
Wonderful marbled effects can be achieved by only partially kneading the colour or coloured pastes together.

To coat a round cake

Prepare the paste by kneading well then shape into a smooth ball.
Place onto the work surface and with a light dusting of icing sugar begin to roll out the paste.
To ensure an even thickness marzipan/sugarpaste spacers

may be placed either side of the paste to roll it out.
Roll out sufficient paste to cover the top and sides of the cake, plus a little extra, as it is always easier to coat a cake if the paste is larger than the actual cake.
Polish the paste with a smoother using a circular motion, this will remove any blemishes, marks and excess dusting sugar.
Place the rolling pin in the centre of the paste, carefully wrap the paste over the pin and lift up onto the cake, positioning as central as possible.
Lay the paste gently over the top and sides of the cake easing any folds or gathers into the excess paste at the bottom.
Ease the paste onto the sides of the cake using a slightly cupped hand and an upwards movement.
Trim the paste to the base of the cake with a palette knife.

To obtain the best finish, use two smoothers one to polish the sides of the cake and the second to hold the cake, firmly in position. Complete the cake covering, by polishing the top edges, taking the smoother from the sides up onto the top surface.

Coating cakes with corners e.g. square, hexagonal & novelty cakes

Always try to roll the sugarpaste out the basic shape of the cake.
Once the paste is over the cake, concentrate on the corners.
Ease the excess paste out at the base of the corner, before using a cupped hand to bring the paste gently into position.
Finish all of the corners before securing any flat surfaces. Trim the paste.
Use two smoothers to bring the paste into a sharper corner shape.

The Use of Colour

When designing a cake, choosing the right balance of colours may not always be obvious and a basic understanding of the principals of colour is always an advantage. The colour wheel or colour circle is the perfect way to illustrate these principles and is the reference point for designers around the world.

Many colours are also used to complement flavours and it is always advisable if using flavours to follow the obvious colour flavour combinations.

White or Cream colour	-	Vanilla
Yellow colour	-	Lemon and Butter
Pink colour	-	Berries e.g. Strawberry
Green colour	-	Lime
Orange colour	-	Oranges
Blue colour	-	Blueberries

Primary Colours
Red, Yellow and Blue
There are only three primary colours and these are the pigment colours from which all other colours are created.

Secondary Colours
Orange, Green and Violet
These colours are created by mixing two primary colours together.

Tertiary Colours
e.g. Red-Orange
A mixture of a primary and secondary colour.

Complementary Colours
These are the two colours located opposite each other on the colour wheel.

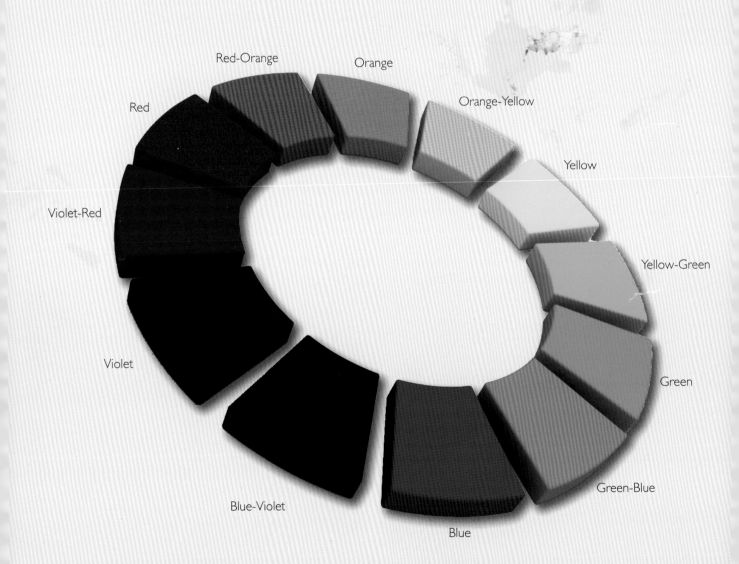

Suggested Quantities of Sugarpaste/Rolled Fondant

As the interest in celebration cakes continues to grow and the ideas and inspirations from around the world blend together, calculating the quantities for basic materials becomes less obvious. The style of design and choice of cake will naturally influence these decisions along with the depth of cake, the thickness of icing and the cake board covering. Therefore these can only be approximate quantities and will require adjusting according to your personal requirements.

The addition of Almond Paste, Apricot Glaze and Buttercream will depend upon the choice of cake e.g. fruit, sponge or cake dummies.

Square Tin	13cm (5")	15.5cm (6")	17.5cm (7")	20cm (8")	22.5cm (9")	25cm (10")	27.5cm (11")
Round Tin	15.5cm (6")	17.5cm (7")	20cm (8")	22.5cm (9")	25cm (10")	27.5cm (11")	30cm (12")
Sugarpaste / Rolled Fondant	500g (1lb)	750g (1lb8ozs)	875g (1lb 12ozs)	1kg (2lb 2ozs)	1.25kg (2lb 8ozs)	1.5kg (3lb)	1.75kg (3lb 8ozs)

A Simple Guide to Approximate Weights & Measure Equivalents

As product packaging and information increases internationally it can be useful to have a list of equivalent measurements, but it is essential to remember that most of these are not an exact equivalent and many have been adjusted for ease of use e.g. the exact metric equivalent per oz varies with some charts using 25g and others 30g per 1oz.

Liquid Capacity *(approximate)*

5ml	1tsp		
30ml	2tbs	1fl oz	$^1/_8$ cup
240ml	16tbs	8fl oz	1 cup
480ml		1pt	2 cups
960ml		1qt	4 cups
1litre		33fl oz	

Weight *(approximate)*

15g	$^1/_2$ oz
30g	1oz
120g	4ozs
240g	8ozs
480g	1lb
1kg	1lb 1oz

Cup Measurements and Metric Weight Equivalents

(approximate)

Please note that these will vary depending upon the type of ingredient

1 cup = 140g Powder ingredients e.g. flour
190g Granular ingredients e.g. sugar
200g Solid ingredients e.g. butter

Baking / Oven Temperatures *(approximately)*

140°C	275°F	1 mark gas	very cool
160°C	325°F	3 mark gas	warm
180°C	350°F	4 mark gas	moderate
200°C	400°F	6 mark gas	fairly hot
220°C	425°F	7 mark gas	hot
230°C	450°F	8 mark gas	very hot

Fun simple novelty cakes can easily be created using basic shaped cakes, which can then either be carved or used in imaginative ways.

Classic designs and textures can provide wonderful opportunities for creativity. For example a traditional basket shaped cake can easily be adapted into a hat, a box or bag for jewellery, makeup, children's toys or fishing etc as well as beautiful designs for wedding and celebration cakes.

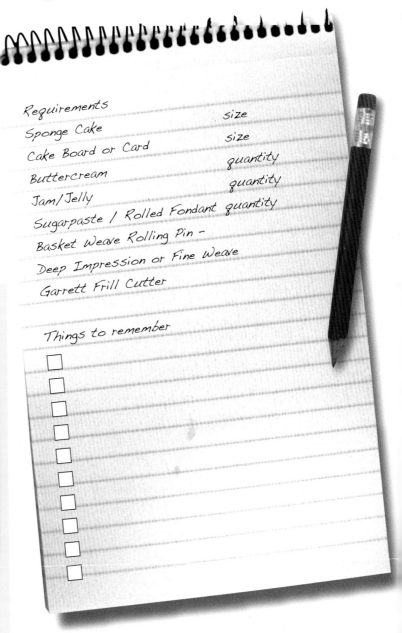

Requirements

Sponge Cake	size
Cake Board or Card	size
Buttercream	quantity
Jam/Jelly	quantity
Sugarpaste / Rolled Fondant	quantity
Basket Weave Rolling Pin - Deep Impression or Fine Weave	
Garrett Frill Cutter	

Things to remember

☐
☐
☐
☐
☐
☐
☐
☐
☐
☐
☐

Basic Techniques and Creative Styling
Simple novelty cake ideas
The use of textured designs and basket
  weave patterns
Frilling techniques, Garrett Frills
  and Flounces

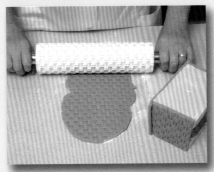

Professional Business Approach
Health and Hygiene
Accounts, Tax and Insurance
Cake Deposits and Payments

Professional Business Approach

The fun of decorating a special cake for family and friends can provide a great sense of personal achievement as well as being the centre piece of a special celebration that brings joy and pleasure for the recipients.

For many cake decorators an interest in creating celebration cakes quickly grows along with the challenge of developing their ideas and skills further. With the encouragement of family and friends this can naturally grow into the possibility of decorating cakes as a business and this is when additional advice can be useful.

The professional business approach pages that are included in all of the PME Professional Diploma modules are designed as a starting point for your cake decorating business and to help as you begin to formulate your thoughts and ideas. The success of any business relies on careful planning, preparation and research and this will vary according to your aspirations, location and budget.

Good Luck and we wish you every success for the future.

Basic Guidelines

Health & Hygiene

It is always advisable to contact your local Environmental Health Officer or Government Officials to obtain information and guidance prior to opening a business. Although a general standard of good practice should naturally be adhered to, specific requirements will vary depending upon your location and this may also include an inspection of your premises and a certification process. It is also recommended that you seek this advice and guidance before committing to any major investments e.g worktops, floor covering or sanitary arrangements etc as this may save time and unnecessary expense.

When handling food it is essential to conform to good food handling standards, but it is also advisable to check as to if you are required to conform to any local or national government regulations or to obtain a particular certificate e.g. Food Handlers Certificate.

Accounts, Tax & Insurance

For many cake decorators understanding and appreciating the finances of running a business may be a new experience and therefore if you are in any doubt contact a local business adviser, tax office, accountant or bank for professional guidance and advice

To ensure that all finances are kept separate from any of your personal accounts it is advisable to open a bank or trading account in your business name. If you are considering applying for trade accounts to purchase materials and equipment it is normal practice for most manufacturers and distributors to request this information prior to assessing your application.

Collect and save all invoices and receipts no matter how small. Request separate VAT or Tax receipts as required by government authorities.

If you are planning on working from home it is advisable to check as to if the running of a commercial business is permitted from your premises. With regards to insurance this will vary depending upon your business and the coverage that you decide is necessary but it is recommended that this also includes a basic Liability Insurance.

Deposits & Payments

Ensure that customers fully understand the payment procedures and requirements for your business. It is not advisable to allow customers to remove the cakes prior to receiving the full payment.

Deposits provide a positive commitment to an order and are strongly recommended, but it is essential to ensure that customers understand as to if this is refundable or non-refundable.
When delivering cakes to a reception, ensure that the full payment has been received in advance or that you have made the necessary arrangements for a guaranteed payment upon delivery.

If you plan to take payments by cheque or credit card it is advisable to seek advice from your bank or financial advisor as to the recommended procedures.

Fabric Effects
Examples of Bows, Drapes, Fabric
Flowers and Ribbons

Lesson 3

In recent years cake designers have embraced the flexibility and softness of appearance that only sugarpaste can provide to create beautiful fabric effects in sugar.

With the addition of either, stitch effects, gentle folds, texture and or a lustre colour, a basic sugarpaste can easily be transformed into a soft flowing fabric that can be used to enhance many celebration cakes.

Basic Techniques and Creative Styling
Coating a cake with corners
Fabric Effects, swags and textured designs
Sugar ribbons and bows

Professional Business Approach
Business Promotion & Advertising
Basic cake recipes
Cake Portions
Cake Pricing

Requirements

Cake	shape & size
Cake Board or Card	shape & size
Buttercream	quantity
Jam / Jelly	quantity
Marzipan or Almond Paste	quantity
Sugarpaste / Rolled Fondant	quantity
Crimpers	
Ribbed Rolling Pin	
Plunger Rose Leaf Cutters	

Things to remember

☐
☐
☐
☐
☐
☐
☐
☐
☐
☐

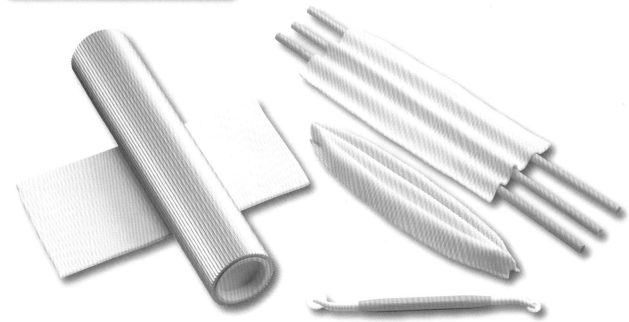

Promotion and Advertising

Most small cake decorating businesses begin simply by personal recommendations and word of mouth and depending upon your hopes and expectations this may attract sufficient customers, therefore additional promotion is not always necessary.

Wedding Fairs

These can be very successful and provide a natural shop window for your cakes.

Basic Tips

1. Prior to booking the space, check if any other cake designers / businesses have also booked and if so how many as this may help you decide as to the suitability. The number will vary depending upon the size of the Wedding Fair.
2. Enquire as to the organiser's plans regarding promoting the fair.
3. Dummy display cakes are to be recommended and will attract a lot more attention than photographs or albums
4. Cake tastings are always popular, although be prepared that they will also be in high demand by visitors that are probably not potential customers. It is advisable to check with your local government authority regarding disclaimers and allergies etc.
5. Networking with your fellow exhibitors may bring unforeseen bonuses. Recommendations from Bridal Shops, Photographers & Car Hire etc.
6. Treat other cake designers with respect.
7. Don't forget to take your business cards and contact details. It may sound obvious but it's easy to forget when you are busy preparing and loading the car for the event.
8. Order Forms / Follow up on Quotations. Although most people will not place an order at the fair be sure to take the full contact details of any potential customers and consider trying to arrange a definite consultation date if possible.

Web Sites - Basic Tips

These are often considered as an essential for any business today, but unless you have the personal expertise, the updating and maintenance may not be cost effective.

Communications must be checked on regular daily basis to ensure customer satisfaction.

Access for customers to most web sites is an easy process and offers the opportunity for them to research and compare with other business's without any pressures.

Newspaper & Magazines - Basic Tips

Placing advertisements in publications can be an expensive process and if possible look for editorial opportunities.
Be sure to check the catchment area and ask for distribution numbers.

There are also many basic simple ways of promoting your business e.g. clubs, groups or schools that your family and friends belong to.

Remember to obtain feed back from your customers by asking them where and how they obtained your business contact details as this will help to give you an indication as to the success of your advertising and promotions

Basic Cake Recipes

Rich Fruit Cake - *round 20cm (8in) or square 17cm (7in)*

butter 175g (7oz)	mixed spice 2 teaspoons
muscovado sugar 175g (7oz)	mixed dried fruit 750g (1lb 8oz)
eggs medium 4	glacé cherries 100g (4oz)
flour plain/all purpose 200g (8oz)	brandy 3 tablespoons
ground almonds 50g (2oz)	

1. Place in a bowl the dried fruit, chopped cherries and brandy. Mix together, cover and leave to stand for a few hours until the liquid has been absorbed.
2. Cream together the butter and sugar until light and fluffy.
3. Gradually blend in the eggs, beating well.
4. Sieve the flour and mixed spice together. Fold into the mixture along with the ground almonds and gradually adding spoonfuls of the dried fruit mix.
5. Place into a greased and lined cake tin. Smooth and level the cake surface.
6. Bake in an oven 140°C (28°F) for approximately 3 hours.
7. To help retain the moisture place a heatproof bowl of water into the bottom of the oven whilst baking.
8. If necessary the top of the cake can be protected by placing a thick card with a hole in the centre, across the top of the cake tin
9. To test if the cake is baked. Insert a skewer to the centre of the cake and remove. The skewer should come out clean.
10. Allow the cake to cool in the pan before wrapping with parchment and foil or plastic wrap.
11. Ideally the cake should be made at least a month in advance to allow it to mature and for the flavours to develop. For additional flavour, brandy can be drizzled over the freshly baked cake or prior to decorating.

Classic Victoria Sponge Cake - *round 20cm (8in) or square 17cm (7in), cup cakes*

butter or margarine 250g (8oz)	self raising flour 250g (8oz)
caster or superfine sugar 250g (8oz)	water or milk 1 tablespoon
eggs medium 4	

1. Cream together the butter and sugar until light and fluffy.
2. Gradually blend in the eggs, beating well.
3. Carefully fold in the flour and flavourings until the mixture is just blended.
4. Place in a greased and lined cake tin. Smooth and level the cake surface.
5. Bake in an oven 160°C (320°F) for approximately 50 minutes.
6. For cup cakes, dispense into small paper/foil cases sitting on a baking tin. Cooking time will be shorter.

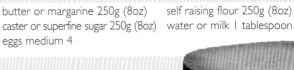

Cake Portion Sizes

It is always helpful to understand and appreciate the approximate number of portions that can be obtained from each cake so that you can advise your customers accordingly.

A portion size will vary, depending upon the choice of cake, but also remember that different traditions and religions can also influence these sizes.

A standard portion size is used when family and friends a given a small taster of cake either at a reception, party or as a gift.

Standard Portion Size

Fruit Cake   2.5cm (1in) square
Sponge Cake   5cm x 2.5cm (2in x 1in)
If the cake is to be cut as for a dessert then these portion sizes may be increased.

Extra Cake Portions

When extra cake portions are required it is accepted practice to recommend additional cutting cakes. These are normally prepared in the same way as the celebration cake, but very simply decorated or just covered with the basic icing. These cutting cakes can then be placed in the kitchen to be served as required.

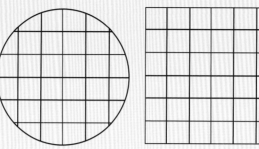

Cake Size	Square Fruit	Round Fruit	Square Sponge	Round Sponge
13cm (5in)	25	16	12	8
15cm (6in)	36	25	18	12
18cm (7in)	49	36	24	18
20cm (8in)	64	49	32	24
23cm (9in)	84	64	42	32
25cm (10in)	100	84	50	42
28cm (11in)	121	100	61	50
30cm (12in)	144	120	72	61
35cm (14in)	196	144	98	72
40cm (16in)	256	196	128	98

Cake Prices

How much should I charge' is probably one of the most frequently questions asked by our students and unfortunately there is no simple answer as this will depend upon so many different factors.

Most cake decorators begin by selling cakes to family and friends and initially are flattered by these early commissions and opportunities to practice and develop their skills. At these early stages payment is often no more than a token gesture or simply enough to cover the cost of materials and therefore does not reflect a true business price.

With all of these thoughts in mind many businesses prepare their own simple formula that can be calculated and used as a basic guideline.

Example - The complete cost of all materials e.g. £45.00 ($45.00) multiplied by three = £135.00 ($135.00) In some businesses the cakes may be sold as a price per portion and therefore the total price would then be divided by the number of portions.

Additions can then be added to this basic pricing guideline depending upon the design, time and skill required.

Progressing to a professional business pricing structure requires careful thought and analysis of many different factors including:

Location . . . . This will affect the prices that are realistically achievable.
Overheads . . . . Including business premises, utilities and staff etc.
Investment Costs . . . . Fixtures and Fittings, including equipment, materials and stock.
Finances . . . . Banking, Tax, Insurance and Financial Advisor etc
Promotion & Advertising . . . . Signs, Stationery, Web Site and Brochures / Price Lists etc
Materials . . . . Cakes, Icings, Boards and Decorations etc
Time . . . . Calculating the time allocated to decorating a cake will also depend upon your
                                                     experience and speed of work.

Recreating in sugar, the beautiful effects of embroderie anglaise naturally allows the designer to reflect the fabrics that are associated with so many special occasions and family celebrations e.g. wedding dress, christening robe and table linens etc.

This lesson is also combined with ideas and techniques to maximise the use of simple cut out shapes creating fun, seasonal and personalised motifs .

Basic Techniques and Creative Styling
Sugar Embroidery and Embroderie Anglaise
Simple cut out cake toppers and motifs
Professional Business Approach
Taking Cake Orders
Good practice and disclaimers
Hiring or renting equipment

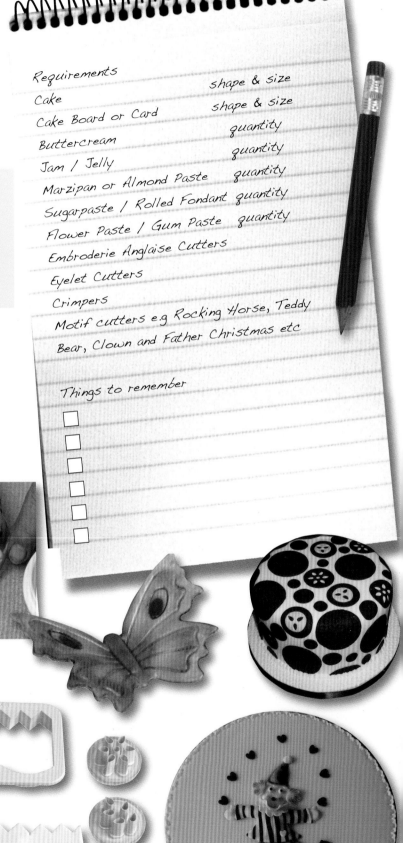

Requirements
Cake   shape & size
Cake Board or Card   shape & size
Buttercream   quantity
Jam / Jelly   quantity
Marzipan or Almond Paste   quantity
Sugarpaste / Rolled Fondant quantity
Flower Paste / Gum Paste   quantity
Embroderie Anglaise Cutters
Eyelet Cutters
Crimpers
Motif cutters e.g. Rocking Horse, Teddy
Bear, Clown and Father Christmas etc

Things to remember

Order Form

This is an example of an order form that can be adapted and developed according to your business requirements.

Hiring or Renting Equipment

The Happy Cake Decorator
Sugarpaste Road
Celebration City
3TC HCD
Tel: 123 456 7890

Customer Name...
Full Contact Address..
....
....Postcode........................
Contact Telephone No: ....Home..........................Work..............................Mobile.................
No of Tiers Required ..One ....Two..................Three ....Four.................Five
Size and Shape of Cake..
Type of Cake Required...
Cake Fillings Required...
Almond Paste / Marzipan ....
Choice of Icing   Sugarpaste / Rolled Fondant ....Buttercream.....................Royal Icing
Colour of Cake Covering..
Additional Colours...
Cake Stand & Knife Required....................................YES.................NO..................
Pillars - Size, Design, Colour & Quantity...
Details of Design & Decoration..

(Additional Details & Drawings on the reverse side)   ....YES..................NO................

Cost of Cake...
Delivery Charge...
Cake Stand Hire Charge...
Cake Knife Hire Charge..
Extras e.g. Top Ornament, Pillars..

TOTAL COST..
Deposit Paid...
Balance Payable...Cash,, Cheque, Credit Card
Deposit for Cake Stand Hire.......................Date Balance Required...............
Date Required for Viewing............................Cash , Cheque, Credit Card
...tion Date ....
...ry Address...Tel No:............................
...ry Date..Time............................

...ners Signature...Date............................
...Full Payment Received...

The Happy Cake Decorator
Sugarpaste Road
Celebration City
CT3 HCD
Tel \No: 123 456 7 890

Cake Stand / Knife Hire or Rental

Hire/Rental Charge of .... is required to hire/rent a cake stand / knife.
us a Refundable Deposit of ....

ake Stands & Knives can be decorated to your individual requirements for an additional extra
harge.

he deposit will be refunded provided that the cake stand and or knife are returned within the
pecified hire dates as per hire agreement.
he deposit refund is also subject to the return of all hired cake stands and knives to be in the
ame condition as to when they were collected, inclusive of all packaging.

he cost of any damage or loss to the cake stand and or knife, including the packaging will be
eaducted from the deposit.

you have difficulties returning any hired items within the agreed specified agreement period,
lease contact us immediately as it may be possible, subject to availability for the hire period to
ae extended.

lease take into consideration that any late returns of cake stands and or knives may result in the
disappointment of other customers.

Hire / Rental Agreement

To hire ....Cake Stand....................Cake Knife......................
Hire Charge..Cash, Cheque, Credit Card
Deposit...Cash, Cheque, Credit Card
Received by..Date.............................

Contact Details of Hirer

Name...
Address ....Postcode................................
Contact Tel No:............................Mobile / Cell No.................................

Terms and Conditions accepted by

Name (Block Capitals) ....Signature...........................
Date........................Date Required...
Date to be Returned.................Date Returned.......................................

Received by ....

It is essential to ensure that customers fully understand the terms of Hire and Deposit. Late or damaged returns may create a knock on effect that can bring problems regarding future customer bookings.

This is an example of a hire agreement that can be adapted and developed according to your own business requirements.

Good Practice and Disclaimers

Most countries have what is often described as a traditional style of celebration cake, but in recent years a wonderful exchange of ideas has seen the development of some amazing cake styles and designs, that have taken cake decoration to a completely different level.

Although this can be exciting it is also essential to balance these ideas with good working practices and to remember that it is also necessary to conform to your governments requirements regarding food handling and materials that come in contact with food.

Most customers will not necessarily be aware of these requirements and will also not understand some of the mechanics and materials that are required to achieve their chosen design and therefore it is essential to take time to explain this information and to be sure that they fully understand.

It is therefore advisable to ensure that your customers are made aware of any not edible items used in the preparation and decoration of all Celebration cakes, Cookies & Cup Cakes etc.

Ideally, try to include with each cake, a disclaimer leaflet, box label or signed document that explains this information in writing.

Example - Please ensure that all pillars, dowels, sugar flowers, posy picks, ribbons, candles and any other non edible items are removed from the cake before cutting and consuming.
Be aware that sugar flowers may contain wires and non edible stamens.

It is also advisable to include a simple statement in reference to nut allergies, similar to those found on commercial packaging.
Example - This product may contain traces of nuts / nut products.

Food colours are a basic essential for all cake decorators, but it is easy to assume that all manufacturers' products are the same and therefore can be used worldwide. Unfortunately requirements for different countries vary and it is essential to check that any food colours that you use conform to your own countries requirements.
e.g. The requirement for the UK is EU listed colours but the USA requires FDA listed colours.

The general advice is ' If in doubt Don't'

Additional decorations e.g. plastic decorations and bride & groom ornaments etc, are also required to meet your own countries food standards and it may be advisable to place a small cake card between the cake and the decoration to ensure that there is not any direct food contact.

Small novelty decorations e.g. toys should also conform to the required toy / food regulations especially those containing small parts. Check the packaging for guidance regarding the safety and minimum age recommendations. Consider adding the information to the disclaimer if necessary.

Ensure that your customer has a copy of any disclaimers, plus if possible, it is always advisable to retain a signed copy for your own records.

Fun modelled figures and miniature cakes

A top Inlay design trimmed with an Embroiderie Anglaise border

Different designs of the Creative Plaque cutters have been used to create both the top and bottom borders

For the cake designer the use of a stacked cake can introduce an interesting and different cake dimension, providing the opportunities for a design that easily flows from one tier to another. This style of cake can also be used to combine different shaped cakes as well as a variety of sizes creating wonderful design opportunities for both traditional and novelty cakes.

In todays society it is also advisable to appreciate that the use of copyright and licensed designs and products may be complex and therefore we have also introduced this as a business element for discussion.

Basic Techniques and Creative Styling
Stacked Cakes and the use of dowelling supports
Textured Sugar Drapes
Simple Figure Modelling

Professional Business Approach
The use of Copyright and Licensed designs and products
Presentation of a multi-tiered cake

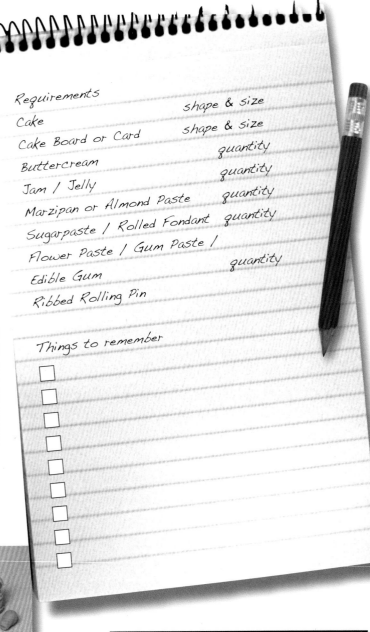

Requirements

Cake	shape & size
Cake Board or Card	shape & size
Buttercream	quantity
Jam / Jelly	quantity
Marzipan or Almond Paste	quantity
Sugarpaste / Rolled Fondant	quantity
Flower Paste / Gum Paste / Edible Gum	quantity
Ribbed Rolling Pin	

Things to remember

The use of Copyright Designs and Licensed Products

This subject is a potential minefield, so the basic advice is to proceed with caution, seek advice and "If in Doubt Don't"
To give you an insight as to the potential pitfalls these are some often asked questions.

Q When a customer requests a cake design exactly the same as one that they have seen in another designers brochure, shop or web site.

To begin with ask the question. Why have they selected your business and not contacted the original designer?

Sometimes the answer is location but on many occasions it simply comes down to pricing and their hopes of purchasing the same cake at a cheaper price.

Remember that the original designer may consider this design to be an exclusive or even their signature design and therefore very protective of their image.

Consider offering to create a cake in a similar style but with additional design features to ensure that cake is especially for them.
Remember to be sure that before you proceed with an alternative design that your customer fully understands and has agreed the new design.

Q Copying cakes from books and publications

It is often perceived that if a cake design is featured in a book or publication, especially if it comes complete with step instructions that it is automatically available for anyone to copy and reproduce for their own cakes.

Unfortunately, especially if the design features a well known character or logo, permission may have only been granted to the author and publisher for their specific use and publication. Therefore it is always advisable to check the individual book listings that are normally located either at the front or back of the book for the full details before proceeding to reproduce the design especially when it is for a cake intended for commercial use or retail sale.

Q Using other designers cake pictures and publications to advertise and promote your business.

This can not only create professional difficulties but also mislead your customers especially when they have placed their order based upon the information that you have supplied.

To protect your own pictures you may wish to consider printing or creating a watermark across the cake using your business name or logo, taking care to ensure that the picture cannot still be cropped to remove the name.

Q Using licensed characters.

Licensed Characters, Logos and Brand Names are often highly protected, and agreements and contracts for their use maybe very expensive and therefore exclusive to a specific company or country and thereby not intended for cakes prepared for retail sale.

You are advised that cake decorators have been prosecuted for the infringement of these agreements.

Presentation of a Multi Tiered Cake

At the early stages of designing a multi tiered cake it is also essential to consider the presentation and although not always visible most cakes will require supporting to obtain the effect required.

Cake Pillars

1. Remember to design the cake taking into account the number of pillars to be used and the space required.
2. Choose the colour of the pillars to co-ordinate with the cake. White pillars can easily be coloured using spray food colours or using a sponging technique
3. Cake pillars can be decorated using piped or simple cut out designs.
4. Clear or crystal pillars can be enhanced by filling with small coloured sweets, ribbons or decorations.

Using Cake Pillars and Dowelling Rods

1. Cake pillars and dowels should be positioned evenly and it is advisable to prepare a pattern to ensure the correct layout.
2. The number required may vary according to the cake shape and size. See the dowelling diagrams.
3. When creating a large cake and to give greater stability it may be advisable to increase the number for the lower tiers.
4. When using dowelling rods without cake pillars, the rods are cut level with the top of the cake.
5. Remember that all cake pillars and dowels must be suitable for food contact.

Traditional Pillars

The dowelling rod is placed through both the pillar and cake, to fully support the cake, from the cake board to the top of the pillar. Mark and cut the dowel level to the top of the pillar.

Spiked Pillars

These are longer pillars that include a shaped section designed to be inserted into the cake and therefore separate dowels are not required.

Spiked Pillars with Rings

These pillars create a traditional effect by simply sliding the separate ring over the spike, to sit onto the cake surface.

Cake Separators

1. These are much larger than cake pillars and can help to evenly distribute the weight of the supported tiers.
2. Clear separators are ideal for filling with sugar or silk flowers.
3. The cake will require supporting with dowelling pegs

Cake Stands

1. Using a cake stand can provide complete freedom of design for the top of the cake.
2. The cakes do not require supporting with dowelling rods.
3. Remember to check the maximum dimensions within the cake stand for both the cake height and width including the cake boards.
4. To create greater interest the cake stands can easily be decorated with ribbons and flowers.
5. Although cake stands are readily available for sale, many specialist shops also provide a hire service. Early booking is advisable to ensure availability.

Stacked Cakes

1. A stacked cake, gives continuity to the cake sides, providing the opportunity for the design to flow continuously from one tier to another.
2. Even though the design may not include cake pillars it will still be necessary to support each tier with dowelling rods.
3. A stacked cake will naturally be heavier to move once it is assembled and extra support can be achieved by using additional cake boards to support the bottom tier
4. The choice of design will determine if the cake can be transported as individual tiers and then assembled at the venue, or if it will require transporting as one complete cake.

Using Cake Spikes or Posy Picks

Non food grade materials should not be inserted into the cake, therefore always use purpose made picks or spikes to hold wired flowers and decorations.

Dowelling patterns

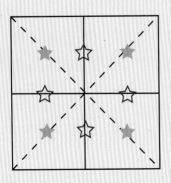  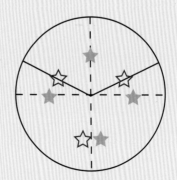 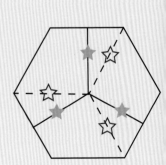

Traditional pillars

Spiked pillars

Spiked pillars with rings

Cake spikes/posy picks

The PME Professional Diploma

PME products are recognised around the world for their quality and innovation and therefore in keeping with these values all PME Professional Diploma teachers and suppliers are required to obtain a PME certificate of approval and authorisation. Our teachers are highly talented and experienced cake decorators and I have provided a space below for you to add your teacher's contact details along with the supplier or location of your course.

PME Professional Diploma Approved Teacher —————————————————————————————

PME Professional Diploma Approved Supplier/Location ——————————————————————————

Address ——

——

Tel No ————————————— Email ——————————————————

Web Site. ——————————————————————

PME regularly participate at selected National and International trade exhibitions and the picture right shows some of our directors and sales team at a recent event.

As you progress through your course you may also wish to personalise your book by adding photographs in the spaces here of your teacher, fellow students or special cakes etc.